HOW TO FIX YOUR WHINE AT WORK

12 Tips to Manage Better and Lead Well

Other Titles By Karl Bimshas

"Leaders Don't Shrug"

"GO GET IT!"

"Pushing Back the Ocean"

"How to Stay When You Want to Quit"

"Disposable Journal"

"Write Advice"

"Perspectives"

HOW TO FIX YOUR WHINE AT WORK

12 Tips to Manage Better and Lead Well

Karl Bimshas

BimMedia

San Diego, California

First Printing 2018

Karl Bimshas Consulting
7676 Hazard Center Drive, Suite 500
San Diego, CA 92108

www.KarlBimshasConsulting.com

ISBN: 978-0-359-14792-2

Dedication

For Katiana and Jonas.

Introduction

Nobody enjoys working with complainers - the people who seem to be perpetually ungrateful and gripe about everything that is wrong. Left unattended their toxicity can contaminate the entire team and organization. So, how can you help them?

Start with yourself first. Make sure you have not been infected with the urge to whine. For example, have you caught yourself complaining about the complainer? It's easy to do. Work can grind you down. Maybe you are feeling overwhelmed or disillusioned. Things are not working out as you planned. You have probably been in your current role for eighteen to twenty-four months - that is when this emotion frequently hits hardest. For some, it comes earlier, for others, much later. Regardless, it's a slippery slope. People begin whining about their job, the people they work with, their family, their weight, their government, their income...

You know; all that whining is unattractive.
There are already plenty of unattractive
people in the world; it does not need more.
Besides, whining is also very annoying. To
help others, take responsibility and show
some self-leadership first.

This guide is an attempt to get you started
in a positive direction. The 12 tips contain
exercises and thought starters aimed at
helping you get over yourself and start
working on something productive. Only
then can you effectively help others. You
will find ideas that you can apply to
virtually any role in any size organization.

Are you ready to take better control of your
attitude and approach toward work and
life?

Let's get going!

Contents

Tip 1: Know Where You Are

Most of the time, you want to look toward the future, but right now, it is best to confront today's brutal facts. At the end of your next workday, answer these questions.

ACTION

❖ How are you feeling?

❖ When you look in the mirror, describe whom you see.

❖ What do you think you sounded like to people who may have overheard your conversations today?

❖ Do you have a sense of purpose in what you do? Why or Why not?

This is your baseline measure. It's subjective, but how you feel after reviewing your answers will give you a lot of information on your current state of happiness and how much energy you will need to devote to improving your outlook.

Tip #2: Get Happy, Stay Happy

Is there anything making YOU happy?

Yes, there is, somewhere. Actively look for something that makes you smile and quickens your pulse. Wouldn't it be cool to feel excited or passionate about something?

ACTION

❖ List three things (or people) that currently make you happy.

❖ How will you spend more time with those three things (or people) that lift your spirits?

❖ You want to feel better, don't you? Then you had better show these people or things some enthusiasm.

Unyielding happiness is unrealistic and unhealthy. Life is full of ups and downs. The goal is to reduce the recovery time it takes every time life deals you one of its inevitable blows.

Tip #3: Check Your Vision

What is the difference you want to make? Something is spurring you on. There's a vision you have that is aching to be realized. Now is the time to breathe some new life into it.

ACTION

❖ What lofty ideal do you want to achieve?

❖ Your vision has to be seen through your eyes first before others can see it. So, make it as vivid as possible. Create a sensible vision. Use all your senses to describe this future state. Keep working on it until others who hear it for the first time easily understand it, memorable, and repeatable.

Too often people spend too much time and energy trying to create a literary masterpiece instead of a clear, easy to follow and understand vision. It's a terrible waste of resources.

Tip #4: Calibrate Your Compass

When you are overwhelmed by the challenges and changes occurring around you, look for the certainties in your life. People who get lost forget to look at their dependable set points on their compass. Pinpoint these directions, and you are never lost. You will know exactly where you are.

If you are currently having trouble, make identifying each personal direction your primary goal.

Discovering where you are essential before you attempt to figure out where you are going next and what vehicle you will use to get there.

ACTION

❖ Calibrate your compass.

- **North** - What are your true values, not the situational ones you use to justify fun?

- **East** - What is your motivating purpose and why do you bother to get up in the morning?

- **South** - How do you rejuvenate and lift your spirits?

- **West** - What do you dream about or want to bring about?

Tip #5: Be a Star, Not a Black Hole

To over generalize, let's say there are three types of people in most organizations.

TYPE 1 - Greatness Inhibitors
Some people feel that what they are doing is just a job. They do not feel like they get enough. In fact, they think they are owed something. They are Greatness Inhibitors, and they suck the oxygen out of the room like a black hole.

TYPE 2 - Potential Stars
Some people wish things could be better. They may not love what they're doing, but it pays the bills, and they still have some ambition and hopefulness about the future. They have had moments of greatness and liked how it felt. These people would benefit from making more contributions to the organization.

TYPE 3 - Highly Valued Stars

The people who often problem-solve away from work and feel that their job enriches a part of their life and part of their life enriches their job are rare. They are the leaders, regardless of title, because they are committed to continuing to perform and enrich themselves and others.

ACTION

❖ Which type of person best describes where you are today? Which do you want to be tomorrow?

Tip # 6: Stop Complaining, Even If It's Fun

People like to tell other people how they've been wronged. So much so, that they have been known to embellish it a little, so everyone knows the pain they are feeling. Sometimes, people unwittingly take on a victim mentality because it provides them with needed attention.

Rather sad, huh?

Think about it. When you hear other people complain at work about their situation, don't you immediately think of all the alternatives that person could have done to avoid their pain? Don't you immediately try to help, even if they don't want to hear your ideas? You never heighten their misery by agreeing with them and encouraging them to give up. You seek reasonable alternatives to buoy their spirits. You have to do the same for yourself.

What or who do you regularly complain about at work?

When you feel lost, and you're floundering, seek out the positive people you know. They are the ones who have modified their attitudes to match new circumstances. Can you identify them? Are they a part of your circle? They need to be. They can be the lifelines that stop you from sinking any further.

ACTION

---

* ❖ Who are the stars in your life that you can chart your success journey with?

* ❖ Try to identify five people who fit the bill of what you need right now. How are you going to spend more time with each of them?

Tip #7: Don't Blame It On Burnout If You're the Arsonist

You may think you are exhausted by work, your boss, life -- and you might be, but don't blame it on burnout if you're the arsonist. People get ticked off when you moan and groan to them about how tired and worn out you feel because they know it's a load of garbage. As a human being, you are capable of sustaining a lot of real pain and hardship. Like it or not, much, much more hardship than you currently feel. Most people you know, have endured more difficulties than you, they just don't talk endlessly about it. You are blessed with a brain that has the capacity to solve almost any problem set before it. Being lazy is a lousy and irresponsible option to pursue.

Decisions can be hard, but you need to do something to address your problems. Fortunately, you have choices.

- You can try to change the problem into something more to *your* liking.

- You can choose to ignore the problem, for a little while anyway.

- You can choose to get rid of the problem. Just move on and find something else.

The same applies to you and your current role. Which do you choose? To change it, ignore it or get rid of it?

Maybe you're frustrated. Sometimes it's hard to get inspired to do anything. One or more of these three things intrinsically motivates people;

1. Personal growth and development,
2. Enhancing an important relationship or,
3. Working on something bigger than themselves and leaving a legacy.

ACTION

❖ Identify what motivates you?

Tip #8: Fix What's Wrong

If you have a, "What difference does it make?" attitude, you need to fix it, right away. It is essential that you find something to start to care about.

When something is wrong and you know it's wrong, or there is a direct or indirect assault on your values, beliefs, mission, goals or people, you need to fight back. Do what is right even if it's not correct. Find a substantial role to play and make a positive difference.

Know that you can make a difference – and in fact, it's your human responsibility.

ACTION

❖ What needs fixing and how will you start?

Tip #9: Beware the Three Donkey Day

Believe it or not, people are generally good. Very few wake up each morning and commit to screwing you in some way. So, beware of the Three Donkey Day. Today, if you find yourself encountering three separate people you feel are complete donkeys; it is probably you who is acting like the ass.

ACTION

❖ When was the last time you came across three "donkeys"?

❖ Reflecting back on that day, who was the biggest donkey? If you believe it was anyone other than you -- think harder. Not sure? Ask someone who was with you.

❖ Knowing what you now know, what will you do differently in the future?

Tip #10: Make a Positive Difference

If you behave glumly every day, it is assured that you will build momentum and speed toward a much deserved outcome. Unfortunately, that outcome will not be a positive one. You're not doomed, but you need to change your approach toward the people you interact with, and it doesn't have to be complicated.

ACTION

❖ As a start, in true servant-leadership fashion, ask others, "What one thing can I do for you that will most help you make a positive difference?"

❖ If possible, fulfill the request right away, or at least help to get it done. Doing this consistently creates a positive and proactive buzz, the likes of which you probably have not seen in quite a long time.

❖ If you ever find yourself lost and rudderless, find ways to make a positive difference.

Tip #11: Know Why You're Still Here

You may feel like giving up, but you haven't yet. Do you know why? Go back to the intrinsic motivators (#7) and ask yourself, "Why am I still here?" Keep probing until one or more of these motivations are revealed.

- Is it For Personal Development?
- Is it Because of the enriching experiences with others?
- Is it to work on leaving a legacy?

ACTION

❖ So, why are you still in your current organization?

Tip #12: Know What You Want

Have you asked yourself, "What do I want?" Do you even know or are you still feeling far off track?

If you've gotten comfortable with your complaining, it's time to stop. Quit playing a victim; it's no way to live. What do you want to do with yourself?

When you were a kid, what did you want to be when you grew up? Why?

Is that still appealing? If not, why not? If yes, why aren't you doing it now?

Think of yourself as an actor on a television show. You want to contribute toward getting high ratings so the show avoids cancellation and you want to be renewed each season. So, you act and perform in a way that leads to the show's success, and you earn awards along the way. Remember, you want to be a Highly Valued Star, not a Greatness Inhibitor.

ACTION

❖ Go ahead; list your ten best excuses for
   not pursuing your dreams. For each one
   ask, "Why is this an excuse?"

❖ Next, figure out how to eliminate each
   excuse. Prioritize this the same way you
   would your goals. You need to get rid of
   the barriers that are keeping you from
   your dream.

Final Thoughts

These 12 tips and series of questions, exercises, and thought starters were aimed at helping you get over yourself and get working on something productive. One of those positive things could be helping others who have not been their optimal selves.

The concepts can apply to virtually any job and any position in any organization. Hopefully, it inspired you to begin moving your mind in a more positive direction.

The intention was to help inspire you to maximize your strengths and continuously improve yourself and your organization by using the powers of vision, passion, and action.

The rest is up to you. It is time to put yourself back in the driver's seat of your career and your life, and begin pursuing the dreams, hopes, and aspirations that you have been moaning about. Believe in yourself and get to work.

About the Author

Karl Bimshas, Boston-bred and California-chilled leadership consultant and author of several books and programs designed for busy professionals who want to manage better and lead well.

With an M.S. in Executive Leadership from the University of San Diego and a B.A. in Mass Communications from Emerson College in Boston, Karl Bimshas has held operational and sales leadership positions in public and private corporations. As a sought-after executive coach and leadership consultant, he's helped busy professionals find, set and get their great goals by discovering the a-ha within.

Want help reducing the whine in your organization?

Karl Bimshas Consulting is the leadership development and accountability firm that busy professionals turn to help grow their confidence and support around management and leadership.

For more information, visit www.KarlBimshasConsulting.com or call 619-497-2670